Falling in Love Again

DAVID & CAROLE HOCKING

HARVEST HOUSE PUBLISHERS
Eugene, Oregon 97402

Scripture quotations are taken from the New American Standard Bible, copyright © The Lockman Foundation 1960, 1962, 1963, 1971, 1972, 1973, 1975, 1977. Used by permission.

FALLING IN LOVE AGAIN

Taken from **GOOD MARRIAGES TAKE TIME**
Copyright © 1984 by Harvest House Publishers
Eugene, Oregon 97402

ISBN 0-89081-621-2

Printed in the United States of America.

Falling in Love Again

DAVID & CAROLE HOCKING

1

Talk to Each Other!

The couple sitting in my office was not getting along. She was doing most of the talking, and he kept insisting that she didn't really love him. She got a stern look on her face, stiffened her jaw, gritted her teeth, and said loudly, "I said 'I love you' once before—do you want me to say it again?"

She was reflecting two sides of the problem of communication: verbal and nonverbal. Her face was revealing to him how she really felt about him. No matter what she said, he just couldn't believe that she really loved him.

Without doubt, communication is the major problem in marriage today. It affects all other problems. If you can't talk about your present problems, you are heading for more difficulties in the future. Many marital partners express great disappointment and frustration over these problems of communication. Most partners confess that their mates do not listen to them.

WHAT KILLS COMMUNICATION?

I've tried to make a list of the things that people have told me in counseling sessions about marriage. What are the basic communication problems which they say are hurting their marriages? I have summarized these into seven problem areas.

Talking Too Much

Many husbands believe that this is a "wife's syndrome," but I have seen plenty of "husband examples" that have convinced me that either partner can be guilty of this problem. One lady told me that her husband's view of good communication is when he does the talking and she does the listening!

Consider the advice of Ecclesiastes 5:2,3,7:

> Do not be hasty in word or impulsive in thought to bring up a matter in the presence of God. For God is in heaven and you are on the earth; therefore let your words be few. For the dream comes through much effort, and the voice of a fool through many words. . . . For in many dreams and

in many words there is emptiness.
Rather, fear God.

Good communication is balanced between talking and listening. You basically are not learning anything when you talk. Some partners hide behind their verbiage and simply do not allow the other partner to share with them. Talking too much is very tiresome, not only for the speaker but also for the person who has to listen. Sometimes the longer you talk the more obvious it is that you don't know what you're talking about!

One man continued to talk in my office for over an hour without a break! He then stopped and asked me why his wife didn't communicate with him! I answered, "Because you talk too much!" He replied, "I don't do that . . . do I?" I learned then that most of us don't realize how much we talk and fail to listen.

Not Saying Enough

The other side of the talking problem is a typical way in which marital partners avoid confrontation—they just don't say anything. Ecclesiastes 3:7 says there is ". . . a time to be silent, and a time to speak." Unless you talk, he (she) will not know what you are thinking or believing, and he will have a tendency to be suspicious of you. He will have a difficult time trusting you if you never share your feelings and thoughts with him.

Many partners try to escape by refusing to talk. To them, what the other partner doesn't know can't hurt. That's where they're wrong! It hurts you deeply when your partner does not respect you enough to talk things over with you.

One man started divorce proceedings simply because his wife wouldn't talk to him. He discovered that she could talk when it came time to divide the estate!

You must learn to talk if you are not already doing it. Do not feel threatened by the other person. Sometimes the verbal abuse we have received in the past keeps us from wanting to try again to talk. But talk we must! Your marriage will continue to deteriorate if there is no real communication taking place between the two of you.

One man whose wife never spoke with him didn't realize that she felt he didn't care about what she had to say. The few times she tried to communicate, he put her down and ridiculed what she was trying to say. As a result she gave up trying.

Sometimes the reasons why one partner is not saying enough are not so obvious. It takes love and understanding by the other partner to resolve this situation. It takes a willingness to change and to begin listening and caring about what your partner feels, thinks, says, and does.

Exaggerations

A common problem in good communication is the matter of exaggerations—making too much out of something. A friend of mine was telling me that his wife called him one day at his office and said, "The whole house is filled with water!" Actually there was a leak in one of the pipes under the kitchen sink, and some water had spilled out onto the floor. He jokingly said to me, "I thought she was talking about a world-wide flood!"

Proverbs 13:3 says, "The one who guards his mouth preserves his life; the one who opens wide his lips comes to ruin." That verse is not talking about an exceptionally large mouth—it is speaking about the problem of exaggeration: "opens wide his lips." Proverbs 22:13 adds, "The sluggard says, 'There is a lion outside; I shall be slain in the streets!' " The undisciplined person has a tendency to exaggerate a situation. Proverbs 25:14 says, "Like clouds and wind without rain is a man who boasts of his gifts falsely."

If you make a practice of exaggerating, your partner has a difficult time trusting you. One wife told me of how embarrassed and shocked she is when her husband tells a story in front of guests that she knows is not true, but is just a great exaggeration. No wonder she is having a difficult time responding to him!

Some people exaggerate to impress others. Other people exaggerate because they don't believe that people will respond to what really happened. Exaggeration can be a terrible habit, and it can seriously affect communication between husband and wife.

Blaming Others

Blame-shifting has been going on since the time of Adam and Eve. Adam blamed Eve, and Eve blamed the serpent (Genesis 3:8-13). When we don't want to accept responsibility, one of the easiest ways to deal with the problem is to blame someone else or our circumstances. Proverbs 25:23 says, "The north wind brings forth rain, and a backbiting tongue, an angry countenance." The common result of blaming someone else is to stir that person to anger. Many marital arguments and fights occur because we blame others instead of accepting the blame ourselves.

Galatians 5:15 warns of the consequences of such verbal attacks: "But if you bite and devour one another, take care lest you be consumed by one another." Verse 26 adds, "Let us not become boastful, challenging one another, envying one another." Some of the sweetest words you can say to your partner are, "I did it . . . I'm sorry!"

One day I walked into our bedroom and said to my wife, "Where did you put those papers I left on the TV?" She replied, "I didn't touch those papers or move them." I responded, "But you had to do it!" She said, "But I didn't do it." I replied, "That's what you always say (bad mistake)!" She answered, "Have you looked in your office?" I said, "No, but it won't make any difference!" I stubbornly went out to my office, and sure enough, the papers were there. I felt stupid, and I knew I had to go into the house and apologize for blaming my wife for my mistake.

Anger

I don't know how many couples say that anger is a major problem, but quite a few remark about it. One man told me that when he gets angry he pounds his fist on the door. I said, "Doesn't that hurt?" He replied, "Yes, but it takes my mind off the thing I was mad about!" One lady throws plates when she gets angry. I asked her, "Isn't that expensive?" She replied, "It's worth it!"

If you want to break down good communication, just get angry—that will do it every time! Proverbs 17:27 says, "He who restrains his words has knowledge, and he who has a cool spirit is a man of understanding." It's hard to keep cool when we verbally attack or blame others. The one leads to the other. Proverbs 19:11 says, "A man's discretion makes him slow to anger, and it is his glory to overlook a transgression." Instead of pointing out your partner's faults and mistakes, learn to overlook them and be forgiving.

But what do you do when you do get angry? Some couples like to fight they say because they enjoy making up afterward! Some anger is justified if it is properly placed. It is right to get mad at sin, but not the sinner. Ephesians 4:26 says, "Be angry, and yet do not sin; do not let the sun go down on your anger." There are times when it is right to be angry, but the real danger comes when we stay angry or shift our anger from a situation to a person. We are never to be angry at *people*. This verse teaches us not to hold things in and stay angry. Don't go to bed angry. Get things straightened out between the two of you before you go to sleep.

Ephesians 4:27 warns us ". . . do not give the devil an opportunity." This means that Satan often uses your anger to cause additional problems. The word "opportunity" is a military term, referring to setting up a base of operations. Don't let the devil do that to you! He would love to make matters worse for you and your marital partner.

Too Quick To Speak

One couple in my office for marital counseling kept interrupting each other before the other person finished the sentence. It was driving me crazy, so I finally said, "Hold it!" I told them that from then on I would allow only one person to speak at a time, and no one could interrupt until the sentence was completed.

Have you ever been talking to someone and wishing that he or she would stop talking so you could talk? Have you ever interrupted someone who was talking to you because you were sure of what he was going to say before he said it? Have you ever been caught doing this, only to find out that you were wrong in what you thought the other person was going to say? Embarrassing, isn't it?

Proverbs 18:13 states, "He who gives an answer before he hears, it is folly and shame to him." Proverbs 25:8 warns, "Do not go out hastily to argue your case; otherwise, what will you do in the end, when your neighbor puts you to shame?'' Proverbs 29:20 puts it in proper perspective by saying, ''Do you see a man who is hasty in his words? There is more hope for a fool than for him.'' Obviously, it is a serious problem to be too quick to speak.

Arguments

One couple I know insists that they have never had an argument. I was in their home on one occasion and watched one of these ''nonarguments.'' When I inquired what they thought they were doing, they both responded, ''Having a friendly discussion!'' I called it an argument.

Have you noticed that no one seems to win in a marital argument? Proverbs 18:19 says, ''A brother offended is harder to be won than a strong city, and contentions [arguments] are like the bars of a castle.'' Proverbs 19:13 says, ''. . . the contentions of a wife are a constant dripping.'' Proverbs 21:9 adds, ''It is better to live in a corner of a roof, than in a house shared with a contentious woman.'' The same principle is stated one more time in Proverbs 25:24. This is obviously an important point—it's tough to live with argumentative people!

Disagreements will exist in any marriage, but when they turn into serious arguments, they are destructive rather than constructive. Arguments occur for many reasons. Sometimes they happen because we have to be right and are unwilling to see the other person's viewpoint. There is a time when we must agree to disagree. We must learn to accept each other regardless of basic disagreements. But what do you do when the husband and wife disagree about a matter in which a decision must be made? This is where God's order for marriage comes in. The husband is responsible to make the decision, and he must then live with it and bear the responsibility for it. That's not an easy assignment! He must carefully consider the wife's viewpoint, ask God for wisdom, and then make the decision, trusting God to reveal in time whether it was right or wrong.

WHAT CREATES COMMUNICATION?

I was impressed one day with a young husband who came in for marital counseling. He was not communicating well with his wife, and he wanted to learn how to do it. He said, "Okay, pastor, I've got about an hour to spare, so teach me how to talk!" Obviously it takes more than an hour to learn how to communicate. Some of the problems that hinder good communication must be resolved first in order for some positive steps to take place. When both partners really want to communicate in a positive way with each other, then things will move along much faster.

It has been helpful to us to work on some things that create good communication. We've come up with the following essentials, and we're sure that others could be added to the list.

Time

Time is necessary to build good communication. Talking to each other on the run is not the way to do it. Quick comments and hurried conversation tend to hinder your ability to communicate effectively.

One of the consistent practices that Carole and I have enjoyed through the years of our married life is to spend at least one day a week together. This is a special time of communicating. We talk about our needs as a family, our children, our marriage, our goals and priorities, our finances, what we expect from each other, and where our hurts and disappointments lie. We have grown so much through these times. We look forward to them every week. That special day is a must with us. It is the "glue" that keeps us close!

Ecclesiastes 3:1-8 is an important passage on "time." It tells us that there is a time for everything and every event under heaven. We need to realize this, and to enjoy the time that we have. We cannot live in the past or the future; *today* is all we have; and we must make the most of it. Take time to talk—it will continue to create good communication and feelings between the two of you.

Honesty

Sometimes honesty hurts, but it's always the best way to go! Never lie to your marital partner. At some point in time you will regret it. Proverbs 19:5 says, "A false witness will not go unpunished, and he who tells lies will not escape."

The Bible is clear about the fact that if you lie you do not love the person to whom you tell the lie. Proverbs 26:28 says, "A lying tongue hates those it crushes, and a flattering mouth works ruin." Flattery is rooted in deceit and lying, and it doesn't belong in a good marriage.

One of the most fallacious viewpoints in marriage counseling is the one which suggests that you do not need to tell your marital partner about your sins. Several years ago a man came over to our house late one evening, and with much hesitation and nervousness he told us that he was committing adultery and could not go on with it anymore. We spent some time going over the passages in the Bible on this subject, and he was willing to repent and to stop the affair immediately. He was in serious emotional turmoil over the whole thing.

In the course of our conversation I suggested to him that he should tell his wife. He reacted strongly to this, telling me that if she knew about it she would leave him. He said he just couldn't do it. I shared with him this verse in Proverbs 28:13: "He who conceals his transgressions will not prosper, but he who confesses and forsakes them will find compassion." He asked me to go with him. I did. His wife was heartbroken, but, contrary to what he thought, she did not leave him, and in time she learned to forgive him for what he had done. Their marriage today is strong and restored.

Some people have told me that if their partner committed adultery, they wouldn't want to know about it. These people do not realize the importance of confession for the benefit of their marital partner. It is always more tragic for a marital partner to find out about a partner's immorality from someone else.

Some words of caution, however, are needed in this regard. We do not believe that it is either wise or necessary for marital partners to discuss in intimate details the sins of immorality which occurred before they ever met. If these former situations have been dealt with properly, confessed, and true repentance resulted, then they should not be brought up again. Also, we believe that things done before one's salvation in Jesus Christ should be buried under His forgiveness. To bring up the past before you were a Christian can only do harm to your present relationship in Christ.

In addition, we believe it to be extremely unwise to share your sinful *thoughts* with your partner in an effort to be completely open and honest. Ephesians 5:12 says, "For it is disgraceful even to speak of the things which are done by them in secret." This verse is speaking about the sinful practices of unbelievers, but by application we believe that it is also dangerous to share what our minds have thought. We are all sinners and capable of very wicked thoughts. We can hurt our marital partners by bringing up these sinful thoughts, especially when they involve people with whom our marital partner is acquainted. We need to learn to bring our thoughts into captivity to Christ (2 Corinthians 10:5).

Trust

A wife called one day, crying on the phone. "Pastor," she said, "I just can't take it anymore. My husband can't be trusted. Whatever I tell him in confidence he shares in public without even asking me for permission or what I think about that!" I've heard that problem many times.

Trust is a wonderful word, and it is essential to a good marriage as well as to good communication. There are two things that are involved. One deals with keeping confidences. Proverbs 17:9 says, "He who covers a transgression seeks love, but he who repeats a matter separates intimate friends." Gossip is a terrible thing, and it is most severe when a marital partner gossips about the other partner. The old sin nature loves to hear gossip! Proverbs 18:8 says, "The words of a whisperer are like dainty morsels, and they go down into the innermost parts of the body."

Marital partners need to keep confidences with each other. Trust means that we can rely upon our partners not to talk about things that we have shared in confidence.

A second thing involved in trust is the matter of dependability. Can your partner rely on you? Proverbs 17:17 says, "A friend loves at all times, and a brother is born for adversity." Proverbs 25:19 adds, "Like a bad tooth and unsteady foot is confidence in a faithless man in time of trouble."

Patience

Love is patient (1 Corinthians 13:4). Proverbs 14:29 says, "He who is slow to anger has great understanding, but he who is quick-tempered exalts folly." Getting angry is often the opposite of patience. Patience means "taking a long time to boil." It is often translated "long-suffering" or "slow to anger." Proverbs 15:18 says, "A hot-tempered man stirs up strife, but the slow to anger [patient] pacifies contention." Patience cools down a potentially dangerous argument. The great value of patience is painted for us in Proverbs 16:32: "He who is slow to anger [patient] is better than the mighty, and he who rules his spirit, than he who captures a city."

I like to get to places on time, and I am usually ready to go a few minutes early, but I have learned not to rush my wife. She likes to know the exact time I plan on leaving, and she doesn't want to be forced to leave any earlier than that. Sometimes I am convicted by my lack of patience when I'm ready to go and I keep pushing her. It doesn't help my ability to communicate with her!

Being patient with your marital partner means that you give him or her time to explain. It means that you understand and are forgiving. While you may be upset with something that happened, it means that you do not transfer that to your partner and express anger. Patience means that you do not set standards of performance that cannot be met. It means that you give your partner time and room to breathe. If you are patient you are not judgmental; you are forgiving and kind. You do not have unrealistic expectations; you are not a perfectionist. You recognize the differences and uniqueness of your partner in relation to yourself.

When I saw how much money my wife spent on a particular item one day, I lost my patience. I pressured her into answering quickly, and she became more nervous and upset. My lack of patience resulted in some bad communication for a few hours, until I asked for her forgiveness. It is easy to jump to conclusions when we don't have all the facts. Sometimes it is embarrassing when our lack of patience proves that we are wrong and have falsely accused our partner. I need to learn to back off and not react immediately to situations about which I am ignorant!

Complete Acceptance

As we sat at a dinner table with a couple that was having marital difficulties, we were amazed at how insecure the wife felt in the presence of her husband. He kept talking down to her like she was a child. He ridiculed her ideas and opinions and then wondered why they were having such difficulty in communicating with each other!

If your partner does not believe that you fully accept him or her, you will have a difficult time communicating with each other. No barrier is quite like that of a lack of acceptance. It is extremely damaging to your self-worth and value. Romans 15:7 says, "Wherefore, accept one another, just as Christ also accepted us to the glory of God." When we realize what this involves, it becomes urgent for us to accept each other without reservation or hesitation.

Forgiveness

Peter asked the Lord in Matthew 18:21, ". . . 'Lord, how often shall my brother sin against me and I forgive him? Up to seven times?' " Jesus responded in verse 22, " 'I do not say to you, up to seven times, but up to seventy times seven.' " Are you willing to forgive when the same offense has been committed several times? First Peter 4:8 says, "Above all, keep fervent in your love for one another, because love covers a multitude of sins." Forgiveness flows out of a loving heart. Colossians 3:13 says, "Bearing with one another, and forgiving each other, whoever has a complaint against any one; just as the Lord forgave you, so also should you."

If you want to hinder communication, just refuse to forgive your partner! Nothing is as devastating to your marriage as an unforgiving spirit. One lady who faced the adultery of her husband with an unwillingness to forgive learned the hard way that her response was not of God. He confessed his sin and truly repented. He ended the relationship with the other woman and earnestly sought the forgiveness of his wife. But she was unwilling. Her bitterness toward what her husband had done to her gave her the justification to have an affair herself. She never realized the damage she had done until it happened to her. Fortunately for this marriage, both partners through much prayer, heart-searching, and good counsel were able to forgive and to restore their marriage.

Forgiveness is essential for good communication. The willingness to forgive is also the refusal to bring the issue up again and use it against your partner. Learn to bury it under the blood of Jesus Christ and His wonderful forgiveness! When you continually bring up a situation that supposedly was forgiven in the past, it reveals a bitter spirit and an unforgiving heart.

So far we have looked at six essentials that will build and create good communication in your marriage. One still remains—the most important ingredient of all. It is *love!* Communication without love is like a lot of noise. Love is so vital to good communication that we have reserved our discussion of it to the next chapter.

2

Say It With Love!

While time, honesty, trust, patience, complete acceptance, and forgiveness are essential for good communication between husband and wife, nothing can compare with the value of love. Love makes our words sweet to the ear and encouraging to the heart. Love helps to express our thoughts when we can't seem to find the proper words.

Marriage is based primarily on *commitment*, not love. But let's face it—the number one reason why most people get married is to experience love. The desire to be loved (admired, appreciated, respected, etc.) is a powerful desire. We often do the wrong thing in order to have someone love us. The bitterness and feelings of rejection that characterize many people today is a direct result of wanting to be loved but not experiencing love or understanding it when they see it.

Agape is the Greek word that describes God's love for us. It is a unique word because it is found often in the Bible but seldom in secular literature. It's a word implying sacrifice. *Agape* love cares about another person regardless of how that person responds to you. It has the ability to respond favorably to those who hate you or treat you badly. According to the Bible, it comes from God. In human terms we might call it "real love"!

Real love is produced by God and demands a personal knowledge of God Himself.

First John 4:7,8 teaches this clearly when it says, "Beloved, let us love one another, for love is from God; and every one who loves is born of God and knows God. The one who does not love does not know God, for God is love." The phrase "love is from God" teaches that God is the source from which this love comes. It does not arise from natural tendency or desire. These verses also reveal that a spiritual birth is necessary before God's love can be experienced in your life.

If you have not experienced a spiritual birth in your life, God's love is not operating within you. We have found a tremendous need in our lives for the love of God. It is the only kind of love that meets our deepest needs and fully satisfies us. In order to have it, you must put your faith and trust in Jesus Christ as your Lord and Savior. He died and paid for your sins; He's alive and coming again! The Bible insists that you must believe these facts in order to be saved (to experience a spiritual birth). When you come alive spiritually, the capacity to love with God's love is finally there.

The first question in all marital counseling sessions deals with one's personal relationship with the Lord. One couple was struggling deeply with their marriage and were ready to end it all in the divorce court. The wife was a Christian and the husband was not, although the wife thought he was. When I inquired about his personal faith in Jesus Christ, he responded that he did not have a personal commitment to God through His Son, Jesus Christ. I asked him if he wanted to become a Christian, and he said yes. From that day in my office until this present time he has been a different man, and their marriage is growing. Your relationship to God makes all the difference in the world. It can be the start of great things for your marriage!

The Bible gives us a great deal of information about God's love. It is obviously quite different from normal human reaction. There's a whole chapter in the Bible dedicated to describing this love (1 Corinthians 13). More beautiful words have never been written!

Real love does not need a response in order to function.

It's easy to love someone who loves you. But what happens when the person you love does not respond to you as you wanted? It's those kinds of responses that lead to major disaster in many marriages. Little things become big things; the hurts get worse, and divorce seems like the only option. But there's a better way— God's love! It responds when the other person doesn't. It forgives and cares when nothing is received in return.

First John 4:10 says, "In this is love, not that we loved God, but that He loved us and sent His Son to be the propitiation for our sins." That's love! We didn't love God first—He loved us! When we didn't care anything about Him, He still loved! Romans 5:8 states, "But God demonstrates His own love toward us, in that while we were yet sinners, Christ died for us." Even though God knows what we are like (sinners), He still loves us! That's what we need in our marriage!

I remember coming home one day from work with romantic notions in my heart. I stopped at the florist and picked up one rose in a vase and got a romantic card. I was anticipating a great response from my wife that might lead to greater things. But when I got home, she was very sick, her hair was in curlers, and she was not very responsive! I realized then that I needed God's love in order to give to my wife without thought of what I would receive in return.

Real love is best seen by what it does.

When will we ever learn? You can say all the right words, but if there's no real evidence in what you do, what you say is hypocritical. At best, you are deceived as to what real love is all about. First John 3:17,18 puts it this way:

> But whoever has the world's goods, and beholds his brother in need and closes his heart against him, how does the love of God abide in him? Little children, let us not love with

word or with tongue, but in deed and truth.

To say "I love you" is needed, but when those words are not backed up with loving action, they seem shallow and even empty.

We tell each other of our love almost every day. We also try to show it outwardly. Physical affection flows between us every day. We don't like to go through a day having not touched each other with love and deep affection. And yet, with all of that, there are times when our love for each other can only be demonstrated by what we do to meet each other's needs. I don't like housework, but I do it anyway because I love Carole. Carole isn't that thrilled about washing my racquetball clothes every other day, but she always does it. These may be small things, but they speak loudly of love.

We try to anticipate each other's needs. It's rare when we have to ask the other person for help. There is a readiness to love. It makes each day exciting! We love to love.

Real love is best defined by its ability to give.

To love is to give, not to get. John 3:16 says, "For God so loved the world, that He gave His only begotten Son, that whoever believes in Him should not perish, but have eternal life." That's love—"He gave." The extent to which God's love gave is revealed in 1 John 3:16: "We know love by this, that He laid down His life for us; and we ought to lay down our lives for the brethren." That "giving" is willing to sacrifice everything for the benefit of the one loved. How we need that in our marriage! Jesus said in John 15:13, "Greater love has no one than this, that one lay down his life for his friends." How far will we go in demonstrating our love?

We both love to give to each other. Somehow there is more joy in giving than in receiving. When Carole's eyes light up over a gift from me, I am blessed. When I'm forced to try on a number of shirts in a store in order to get that right one that Carole wants to buy for me, she gets excited. In Acts 20:35, the apostle Paul told us to remember the words of Jesus when He said, ". . . It is more blessed to give than to receive." How true that is!

But when love is not the motivation, giving to others can be a burden instead of a blessing. It hurts when people do not respond to your gift with at least a sincere "thank you." However, God's love can keep giving even when that happens. There are people we all know who will not respond favorably no matter what you give them. We must learn to love them with God's love, for they desperately need it.

One of the "fun things" you can do is to buy a little gift when there is nothing to celebrate—no birthday or anniversary—just a little gift to say "I love you." It doesn't have to be expensive or flattering. Love gives!

Real love is developed by obedience to God.

This is one of the most important truths you can ever learn about experiencing the love of God. First John 2:5 says, "But whoever keeps His word, in him the love of God has truly been perfected . . ." In John 14:15 Jesus said, "If you love Me, you will keep My commandments." First John 5:3 puts it this way: "For this is the love of God, that we keep His commandments; and His commandments are not burdensome." The real test as to whether we are loving with God's love is our obedience to what the Bible says.

When a married man decides to commit adultery because he has become involved with another woman besides his wife, he is not loving no matter what he says. He might justify his actions by saying that he loves the other woman. There is a sense in which he might be telling the truth—it is a kind of sexual love. But it is *not* the love of God. He has just demonstrated his lack of God's love for both his wife and the woman with whom he had this affair. If he really loved both of them, he would respond with obedience to God's Word. He would resist having sexual relations with the woman who was not his wife, and he would remain faithful to his wife and have sex with her only. This doesn't mean that he did not have sexual feelings or desires for the other woman. But it does mean that his love controls his desires. His love comes from God; it walks in obedience to God regardless of how he feels.

A young husband talked to me one day about wanting to leave his wife because he loved another woman. I told him that it was not God's love that he was experiencing, but lust. He got angry and said that he knew love when he felt it. I replied that love isn't based on feelings but on commitment and obedience. He then told me that he no longer "felt" any love for his wife. I responded that if he would return to his wife and be obedient to God's commandments, his love for his wife would grow. After several weeks of confrontation, he went back to his wife, confessed his sin, and sought her forgiveness. Within a matter of weeks he shared with me that his love for his wife was beginning to grow again.

Real love is hindered by sin in our lives.

When a certain wife told me of how her love for her husband was diminishing, I was concerned and inquired what was happening. She blamed him for many things, and told me that she was not being fulfilled by her husband. When I asked if there were any other men in her life, she became hostile, and when she finally calmed down, she admitted that there were other men. Sin hinders real love.

The one thing that will stop the flow of God's love in the believer's life is sin. First John 3:11,12 makes this quite clear:

> For this is the message which you have heard from the beginning, that we should love one another; not as Cain, who was of the evil one, and slew his brother. And for what reason did he slay him? Because his deeds were evil, and his brother's were righteous.

Cain did not love his brother, Abel. The reason? Cain's deeds were evil. It was *sin* that hindered the love of God from being demonstrated

toward his brother. Sin grieves the Holy Spirit of
God, who produces the love of God in our hearts
(Romans 5:5; Galatians 5:22). When there are
sinful attitudes and practices that are dominat-
ing our lives, it is impossible to love our marital
partner the way God intends us to do.

The sin in our hearts may be attitudes toward
other people and not just between each other.
These wrong attitudes make it extremely difficult for us to respond to each other with God's
love. Until we get the sin confessed and forsaken, we struggle with loving each other. The
sin (however small it may seem) stands as a
barrier between us, hindering us from enjoying
God's love and each other.

My anger toward our children was hindering
our relationship one day, and I became very
unloving toward my wife. She said in a sweet
way, "Honey, don't take it out on me also!"
Without realizing it, I was unloving toward my
wife because of my anger toward my children.
Until I apologized to my children, the love of
God was not evident in me.

*Real love is based on a strong commitment
that can withstand all pressures and attempts to
destroy it.*

Without God's love, it is not surprising that so
many marriages do not survive, but end up in
divorce. Song of Solomon 8:6,7 puts it beauti-
fully:

> Put me like a seal over your heart, like
> a seal on your arm. For love is as strong

as death. . . . Many waters cannot quench love, nor will rivers overflow it. . . .

Marriage will be tested. But the cement that keeps it together is a strong commitment produced by the love of God. There will be "waters" that will come from time to time that try to quench the flame of love between husband and wife. Sometimes it is another woman or man. But God's love keeps the marriage strong. His love refuses to accept any substitutes.

When failures and disappointments come, don't let them drown your marriage. God's love is ready and willing to forgive. First Peter 4:8 says, "Above all, keep fervent in your love for one another, because love covers a multitude of sins." When you dwell on the other person's faults and weaknesses, you are not loving. Love covers rather than exposes. Many hurts have to be buried in the love of God. The past must be forgiven and forsaken. Don't let past failures affect the level of commitment you have to each other. Determine in your heart to love the other partner regardless of his or her faults, sins, and weaknesses. After all, God loves you even though He knows all about you!

3

When Your Partner Does Not Respond!

The woman in my office that day was deeply frustrated. She said, "My husband never responds to me. I've tried everything. He remains cold and indifferent to me and seldom says anything of value or concern to me. It really hurts, and I can't take it anymore." Her tears were exchanged for anger during the course of our conversation. She was bitter toward her husband for the way he was treating her.

What advice should we give to a person who is deeply concerned over the failure of a spouse to respond? One lady writes her husband notes. She puts them everywhere, begging him to talk to her about her needs and concerns. Some resort to shouting and displays of anger. Some, unfortunately, seek other partners. What should a person do?

Don't Panic!

One of the first things to do is to relax. That may sound like no answer or simply indifference. But, that's not the point. I have observed that people often panic and do stupid and foolish things that they later regret. Our anxiety often reveals our lack of trust in what God can do. God's power is great, and He can change an unresponsive partner.

According to the Bible, God is in control of the events and circumstances of our lives (Romans 8:28). We need to trust Him. That doesn't mean we do nothing, but it does mean that we talk to Him about it. Prayer is your most powerful weapon, not your last resort! Philippians 4:6,7 teaches us:

> Be anxious for nothing, but in everything by prayer and supplication with thanksgiving let your requests be made known to God. And the peace of God, which surpasses all comprehension, shall guard your hearts and your minds in Christ Jesus.

Can you thank God for the situation and trust all your anxiety to Him? First Peter 5:7 admonishes us, ". . . casting all your anxiety upon Him, because He cares for you." What a great comfort! So relax! God is in control, and there's a reason for everything that you are experiencing. It may not be clear to you now, but one day it will.

It is important to be patient for God's timing. Galatians 6:9 reminds us:

> And let us not lose heart in doing good, for in due time we shall reap if we do not grow weary.

The Lord is working His plan in our lives. His timing is always best. Be patient. As tough as that sounds, recognize that God must change your partner. Psalm 27:14 advises:

> Wait for the Lord; be strong, and let your heart take courage; yes, wait for the Lord.

It's so hard to wait, especially when you're hurting. Relaxing, when the tension between marital partners is still there, is pretty hard to do. But, do it we must!

Understand the Situation from Your Partner's View

Jesus warned us in Matthew 7:1-5 about seeing the other person's problem while ignoring your own:

> How can you say to your brother, "Let me take the speck out of your eye," and behold, the log is in your own eye? You hypocrite, first take the log out of your own eye, and then you

will see clearly enough to take the
speck out of your brother's eye.

Jesus promised us that we would "see clearly"
if we considered our own problems first. Your
partner may be unresponsive because of something you have done, said, or neglected to do or
say.

Unless we try to understand the situation
from our partner's point of view, we may jump to
some wrong conclusions. Many marital partners
are unresponsive because they have been hurt by
the other partner at some point. Maybe they tried
to communicate, but were rejected or put down.

Communication might also be difficult for any
of the following reasons:

- Limited vocabulary
- Personality and temperament differences
- Critical attitudes expressed by partner
- Judgmental spirit of partner
- Physical exhaustion or illness
- Poor self-image (feeling that you
  have nothing worth sharing or that
  your ideas and opinions are not val-
  ued or wanted)
- Lack of common interests (nothing
  to talk about)
- Inability to listen (frequent complaint!)

Sometimes unresponsiveness is related to
hurts of the past. One wife, whose husband

stopped going to church and never read his Bible or prayed with his family, was surprised to learn that her husband was deeply offended by another church member several months previously over a matter that he simply did not share with her. Things got worse. His wounded spirit was controlling his response. When he and the other individual finally got together and the matter was resolved and forgiveness applied, his interest in spiritual things was restored.

Love Without a Response

In the last chapter, we dealt with the matter of communicating love. We desperately need it if our marriages are to be what God wants them to be and we need them to be. In our opinion, one of the greatest needs when dealing with unresponsive partners is to reinforce the principle of loving your partner without expecting a response. There is something very selfish about wanting your partner to change. We get greatly concerned over the lack of response and it sometimes reads out to our unresponsive partner as a lack of love. We only love when there's a response.

Do we really believe that it is better to give than to receive? How many of us are motivated by what we can do for our marital partner? It hurts when there is little or no response, but does that mean that we stop loving? No! That's the time when love really declares itself. That's when we learn how strong it is. If you are married to an unresponsive partner, don't get frustrated and decide to give up! Start making plans to love your partner without expecting a response in return. That's what God's love is all about!

We believe that the number one need in communication is love. Partners won't communicate properly when there is no love. Love heals when everything else has failed. Loving your partner like the Bible teaches can revolutionize your marriage and cause your partner to want to respond.

When the atmosphere between the two of you is one of suspicion, tension, judgment, criticism, hostility, etc., then very little communication will take place. Real love breaks down barriers and walls of resentment. It encourages talk and the desire to listen. It cares about the other person and wants to know how he or she thinks and feels about everything. The atmosphere of love can make the most unresponsive partner want to talk and share and give. May God help us all to understand this!

Let's Take Inventory

Here is a series of questions that you might ask yourself or discuss with your marital partner about communication, including its problems and essentials.

To the Husband:

1. Do you have special times when you and your wife are alone and talk? When?
2. Do you listen to your wife and does she know that she has your undivided attention?
3. Are there subjects that you cannot discuss with your wife? Why?
4. Do you enjoy talking with your wife?
5. Do you look directly at your wife when you talk to her?
6. Do you make her feel that her opinions and beliefs are important and valuable?
7. Do you interrupt her before she has finished speaking?
8. Do you show interest in the activities of your wife? Do you ask her questions about what she is doing or what she likes?
9. Does your wife feel that she can talk with you about anything without being judged or put down? If not, what would you do to change that?

To the Wife:

1. Are you sincerely interested in what your husband enjoys talking about?
2. Do you pay attention to him when he talks to you?
3. Do you look at him directly when you are talking to him?
4. Are there subjects that you cannot discuss with your husband? Why?
5. Are you relaxed in talking with your husband? Do you get uptight?
6. Do you make your husband think that you want something from him when you talk to him?
7. Does your husband believe that you enjoy talking with him?
8. Are there unresolved issues between the two of you that make communication difficult? What should you do about it?
9. Would you rather talk with your husband about a matter before you speak with anyone else? If not, why do you talk to others first?

Let's Get Started

The preceding questions may have stimulated you and encouraged you to develop a deeper and more intimate communication with your partner. What steps should you take now to keep the communication lines open and growing?

1. Set aside a definite time each week for communication between yourself and your marital partner. Make it an appointment and write it on your calendar. Don't let other things rob you of this time!
2. Learn to ask questions of your partner. Get out of the habit of telling your mate what you want or think. Start learning about your partner's feelings, desires, and ideas.
3. Learn to talk privately, away from the children. Don't argue in front of your kids! Whenever a problem comes up, learn to say, "Let's go to our special place for a private talk!"
4. Say something nice and loving to your partner every day. Begin the day with "I love you." Show appreciation to each other before you go to bed at night.
5. Speak quietly. Whenever you raise your voice, the chances of bad communication always increase.
6. Always consider your partner's reasons. Find out "why" and you will understand better how to communicate the next time.

7. Learn to pray together as well as separately. If you can talk to God about it, you will have a better chance of talking to each other with love and understanding.

About the Authors

David Hocking is pastor of Calvary Church of Santa Ana and the radio Bible teacher on the "Biola Hour." Dr. Hocking has written several books, including *Good Marriages Take Time* and *Romantic Lovers*, both coauthored by his wife, Carole.

The Hockings—married since 1962—have three children and draw upon their years of marriage and family life to provide practical and down-to-earth insights in their books.

Other books authored by David Hocking include *Pleasing God*, *Are You Spirit-Filled?*, and *Be a Leader People Follow*. All of the Hockings' books are available through the "Biola Hour."